A Different Way To Die

A play

Lynn Brittney

GW00640744

Samuel French—London
New York-Toronto-Hollywood

30130 120942106

Please see page iv for further copyright information

CHARACTERS

Anna Gruber, thirty
Magda, about twenty
Dr Feldman
Joseph Gruber, thirty-five

The action takes place in a hotel room in Jerusalem

Time – 1950

A DIFFERENT WAY TO DIE

A hotel room in Jerusalem in the newly-created state of Israel, 1950

It is a fairly spartan, modernistic room. There is a single bed with a bedside table, on which is a gas mask container. Downstage there are two armchairs facing each other and a low coffee table. The window looks out over the street and is criss-crossed with paper tapes, to prevent the glass splintering in the event of an explosion

As the CURTAIN *rises we hear the sound of a key in the lock. The door opens and Magda enters, followed by Anna. Magda, about twenty years old, is dressed in very summery clothes, a pair of trousers and a short-sleeved shirt. She is carrying an automatic weapon slung over her shoulder on a strap. Anna, aged thirty, is blonde and is wearing a high-necked blouse and a winter-weight skirt. She is carrying a raincoat, a handbag and a small suitcase which she places on the bed during the opening conversation*

Magda (*off-hand*) This is where you will be staying for the moment ...

Anna For the moment?

Magda Until we go through the necessary formalities.

Anna Oh, I see. What, exactly, are the necessary formalities?

Magda Dr Feldman will explain them later.

Anna (*alarmed*) A doctor! I said I didn't want to see a doctor.

Magda Feldman is a psychiatrist. He just wants to talk to you.

Anna Why?

Magda I don't know, you'll have to ask him.

*There is silence. Anna begins to unpack her case on the bed.
Magda looks out of the window*

Anna You don't like me very much, do you?

Magda I beg your pardon?

Anna I said, you don't like me very much, do you?

Magda (*slightly embarrassed*) I'm sorry, I don't understand
what you mean.

Anna (*smiling ruefully*) Ever since you met me at the airport you
have been distinctly cool. Not that it bothers me, you understand.
There are worse things in life than being disliked. I was just
curious as to why, that's all.

Magda (*offhand again*) Forgive me but I think you must be
mistaken. I am merely doing my job. I have no personal
feelings one way or the other towards you.

Anna No? Then perhaps all you young Israelis just have a cold
manner. Perhaps that's what people are like in hot countries. I
don't know, I've never been outside of Germany.

Magda (*defensively*) We don't have time for emotions here. It's
best not to make too many friends. They might get killed the
next day.

*Anna lights a cigarette and puts the packet down on the coffee
table during the following*

Anna There should always be time to make friends. Even in the
death camps people made friends.

Magda (*sharply*) Please don't talk about those things.

Anna Oh, I'm sorry. Were you in a camp too? I'm sorry.

Magda No, I was never in a camp. My family have lived here for
three generations, since the Russian pogroms in the last century.
First we were Palestinians, now we are Israelis.

Anna And always Jews.

Magda No. *You* are a Jew — *I* am an Israeli.

Anna There's a difference?

Magda Of course.

Anna I must be dense. Explain it to me.

Magda Israelis fight, Jews don't.

Anna Ah. Now I understand.

Magda Understand what?

Anna Why you don't like me. I've seen it before, except it was from Germans.

Magda begins to protest

(*Interrupting*) No, I don't mean Nazis — that was hatred. No, I mean the ordinary Germans after the war. They didn't like me because I was a camp survivor — a reminder of their guilt.

Magda I don't feel any guilt.

Anna No, of course you don't. You don't like me because you can't understand how I could let myself be put into a camp, can you?

Magda (*quietly*) No.

Anna I've seen that before too, from the odd Jew who didn't get put in a camp because they were able to pretend they were a Gentile, or because they managed to escape before the rounding–up started. Don't worry, I don't take it personally, because I don't really understand it myself.

Magda What do you mean?

Anna Well, I had my moments, before the camp, during, and particularly afterwards, when I couldn't understand how we let it happen to ourselves. Particularly how we let it happen to our children. I've never had any children — and I won't now — but I always thought that if I had been a mother I would have done anything to keep them out of the camps.

Magda (*thawing*) Yes. You're right. I can't understand it. Day

after day, I see people here, in the streets, with numbers on their
arms. It makes me want to scream at them. Six million Jews:
how could anyone kill that many Jews without meeting any
resistance? Here, we fought all the time, to get independence
and to keep it, against enormous odds. I can't understand what
happened in Germany, no matter how hard I try.

Anna No-one can understand unless they were a part of it, and
even then it's hard. Mass hysteria, lies, bad leadership, it all
played a part. People like me try to justify it by saying we were
too young and we didn't know, but even that doesn't work.

Magda It frightens me too.

Anna Frightens you? Why?

Magda Because I think, sometimes, that maybe it's a part of the
Jewish character just to give in without a fight. So many
persecutions through the ages and nobody ever fought back.
I'm frightened because I think it might eventually take over this
country and then the Arabs will really drive us into the sea.

Anna And an influx of people like me only adds to your worry,
is that right?

Magda Yes.

Anna And it makes you feel guilty because you don't want us
here?

Magda Yes.

Anna Don't you think that those who survived the camps might
have a burning desire to live and want to fight alongside you?

Magda Do you think so?

Anna Speaking for myself, I'm not sure. The scars are deep and
I am still in a sort of dream state. I cannot get out of the habit
of only thinking about one day at a time. And I am too totally
absorbed in myself to be of much use to any organization. But
maybe that passes. And maybe we survivors rejoin the human
race when we feel we can and then, maybe, we can do our bit.
(*She looks at Magda with pity and takes her hand*) I wouldn't

worry. Your new nation will survive. After all, you have one advantage that we never had. (*She points to Magda's gun*) Guns.

Magda You're a nice lady. I'm sorry I was so unpleasant at the airport. Let me make it up to you. I'll take you shopping later if you like. You need some lighter clothes.

Anna (*uncertainly*) Thanks, we'll see. I may not be staying ——

A knock at the door interrupts Anna. Magda goes to the door and opens it

Dr Feldman enters. He carries a briefcase

Dr Feldman (*irritatedly*) Magda! Where's Elizabeth? I thought she was meeting Mrs Gruber.

Magda Elizabeth's ill. I had to take over at the last minute.

Dr Feldman I've told you that I don't want you doing reception work. You don't have the right attitude. (*To Anna*) Mrs Gruber, I'm sorry if Magda has been rude at all. You must forgive our young people their insensitivities. (*He moves forward and shakes Anna's hand*)

Anna Not at all, Doctor. Magda and I have got along very well.

Dr Feldman (*puzzled*) Oh. Well, good. Mrs Gruber — may I call you Anna?

Anna Please.

Dr Feldman Anna, I have some wonderful news for you.

Anna Really? You have found a place for me to live?

Dr Feldman Better than that. I think you had better sit down.

Dr Feldman gestures to one of the armchairs; Anna sits in it and Dr Feldman sits in the opposite chair

Anna, when people apply to emigrate to Israel there are many

investigations that have to be done, not the least of which are
whether the applicant has any relations in the country already.

Anna (*flatly*)I have no relatives whatsoever.

Dr Feldman Ah, well, there you are wrong. Mrs Gruber,
we have found your husband.

There is silence. Anna, not moving, looks stunned

Er ... did you understand, Anna? We have found Joseph, your
husband.

When Anna speaks she sounds as if she is choking

Anna My husband is dead ... it's impossible.

Dr Feldman Your husband is very much alive, Anna, although
he is far from well. He has been ill since he arrived in this
country three years ago. (*He takes some papers, a notepad and
a photograph from his briefcase*) He came in on one of the
illegal immigration ships, while the country was still under
British mandate. I'm afraid he was wounded by a British bullet,
which did not add to his state of health. He was hidden by an
Israeli family and then taken into a hospital after independence,
where he has remained until now. (*He hands Anna the
photograph*) This is the photograph. As you can see he is
unwell and has aged considerably, but apart from that he should
be recognizable to you.

*Anna stares at the photograph and then clutches it to her and
begins to cry*

(*Getting up to comfort Anna; rather awkwardly*) It's all right,
Anna. I know it must be a shock. Everything will be all right.

Magda Shall I fetch some tea?

Dr Feldman Yes, yes, a good idea.

Magda exits

Anna, perhaps you would feel better if you lay down on the bed.

Anna (*shaking her head*) No. I'll be all right. It was just seeing his face ...

Dr Feldman Yes, of course. I can give you a tranquillizer if you wish. I have my bag here.

Anna No, no drugs.

Dr Feldman I understand. Magda has gone for some tea. A hot sweet drink will help. Have you a cardigan or something to put round your shoulders?

Anna (*gesturing towards the bed*) My raincoat, over there.

Dr Feldman fetches the raincoat and drapes it round Anna's shoulders

(*Looking at the photograph again*) He looks like his father. So much like his father.

Dr Feldman I'm afraid his illnesses have been a great strain upon his system.

Anna Is — is he dying?

Dr Feldman No. He has had various health problems. But, like many survivors, his state of mind has much to do with his powers of recovery. He has improved greatly since he learnt that you were alive.

Anna (*horrified*) He knows I'm here?

Dr Feldman Well, yes, of course. He contacted the authorities when your name appeared in a list of immigration applications in the newspaper.

Anna You list them in the newspaper?

Dr Feldman Please understand, Anna, it is the most important information to most people in Israel. Everyone, with few exceptions, is searching for a long-lost relative. Most hope in vain that a member of their family may have survived. So many people came out of the camps and scattered over Europe. The Allied authorities really couldn't do an efficient job of detailing all the survivors. In fact you were one of those that slipped through the administrative net. We had terrible trouble verifying your existence after nineteen-forty. It was only because of your husband that your application was granted. But, even so, I have to ask you some more questions about the missing years.

Anna Why? I was in a camp, I survived. What more is there to say?

Dr Feldman Try to understand, please. We have had many instances of individuals assuming the identities of dead people in order to get into this country.

Anna Why would anyone want to do that?

Dr Feldman takes a newspaper from his briefcase and shows a photograph in the paper to Anna

Dr Feldman Have you ever seen this man before?

Anna No, I don't think so. Why?

Dr Feldman Take another look, Anna. This man was a *kapo* at Thereisenstadt from nineteen-forty-two to nineteen-forty-five. He personally assisted the Nazis to exterminate his fellow Jews for three years, in return for his own life and minor rewards. He assumed the identity of one of his dead colleagues in order to get into this country. Foolish really. He was recognized on his third day in Tel Aviv by a survivor of the camp. As you can see from the newspaper, he is now facing a public trial. Weren't you at Thereisenstadt?

Anna Not after nineteen-forty-one.

Dr Feldman Ah. That explains the trouble we had. Your husband knew you had been taken there and he thought you had died there. The Russians captured some of the records of the camp, but the Nazis had managed to destroy the records of the early years, so we didn't know whether you had really survived or not.

Anna Must we go through this now? I'm tired and I need to think.

Dr Feldman I'm sorry, Anna. But we have only forty-eight hours in which to establish the facts and for your husband to sign a deposition stating you are indeed his wife. Otherwise, your immigration papers will be rescinded.

Magda enters with tea things on a tray. She sets the tray down on the coffee table

Magda (*picking up the cigarette packet*) Cigarette, Mrs Gruber? Is that all right, doc?

Dr Feldman (*starting to pour the tea*) Yes. Magda, I think you had better leave us alone now.

Anna No! I think she should stay. There are things to be discussed which may help her to understand things more clearly.

Dr Feldman I'm sorry?

Anna Never mind. Just let the girl stay. It will be good for her education.

Dr Feldman As you wish. (*He hands Anna a cup of tea*) Do you feel up to continuing?

Anna Go ahead.

Throughout the following interrogation Dr Feldman is kind, softly spoken but insistent and probing

Dr Feldman Where did you go from Thereisenstadt?

Anna To another camp. I don't know where it was or what it was called.

Dr Feldman You don't know? Surely, the camp had a name. Even if you didn't know where it was, it must have had a name.

Anna I — I was ill for a long time. I don't remember anything very much. It was in Poland, that's all I know.

Dr Feldman Surely you were not ill — so ill you couldn't remember for four years?

Anna I was — ill — afterwards. It was then that I couldn't remember.

Dr Feldman (*unconvinced*) I see. How did you manage to end up in — (*he looks at his papers*) — where was it — Munich?

Anna I — just did.

Dr Feldman Were you liberated from your camp by the Allies?

Anna No. That much I do remember. We were just released — by the Germans ——

Dr Feldman The Germans!

Anna Well, released is perhaps not the right word. There was a lot of activity one night. Lots of trucks arriving and a big bonfire in the courtyard. Papers being burnt, that sort of thing. Then, in the morning, there were no more Germans. They had gone.

Dr Feldman Then what happened?

Anna We all just sat around. We knew that the gate was open. It was wide open, we could all see that. But none of us dared move. I don't know — I think we thought it was a trap. That if we stepped outside they would machine-gun us down or something. Anyway, we just stayed there, for two or three days, I think. And then some nuns came and told us that the Germans had retreated and the Allies were only five kilometres away. So I got up and went.

Dr Feldman Why didn't you wait for the Allies?

Anna (*bitterly*) Soldiers were soldiers as far as I was concerned. I didn't know that any uniform was better than any other. I just wanted to get away.

Dr Feldman Where did you go?

Anna I don't know. I just started walking and then, at some point, I collapsed. Someone must have found me because I woke up in a hospital. I stayed in the hospital a long time because I couldn't remember who I was or where I came from. Then when some of my memory came back, they let me work in the hospital for a little money. I saved the money and went to Munich.

Dr Feldman Why Munich?

Anna I didn't want to go back to Dusseldorf. I didn't want to look at the streets where I had spent my childhood. I went to Munich because I had had some relatives there.

Dr Feldman What relatives?

Anna My mother's sister and her husband.

Dr Feldman (*making notes*) And you lived with them.

Anna No. They were dead. They had been taken too. So I just found a room and got a job.

Dr Feldman Doing what?

Anna In a bar. Look, I can't tell you any more. Can't we leave this?

Dr Feldman I am sorry but I have to be sure that you are who you say you are. I have to make a full report to the authorities.

Anna (*bitterly*) I thought I was done with all that.

Dr Feldman Sorry?

Anna Being documented, being processed. Whatever you want to call it.

Dr Feldman I'm sorry. Would you like some more tea? (*He signals to Magda*)

Magda comes to the table and pours Anna some more tea

Can we go back to when you were first taken to the camp? Thereisenstadt I mean.

Anna (*sighing*) If you wish. You know what was so curious for me was that that was the year that I first realized I was Jewish. I mean, that it was something different from being German. My

family were not religious, you see. My father was a scientist
and I think really that he was an atheist. We never kept the
Sabbath or anything like that. We lived in a scientific community.
My parents' friends were from all religions and backgrounds.
But, in nineteen-forty, I met and married Joseph — and
Joseph's family were religious. I don't know why I fell in love
with him. We were so different. He was serious, very Jewish,
a scientist like my father — that was how we met. I, on the other
hand, was frivolous, liked to have fun, you know. Joseph's
mother had to teach me how to be a Jewish wife and I found it
very hard. *My* mother was furious. She said I was turning into
a subjugated woman. My mother was very independent. It was
through Joseph's family that I became aware that Jews were
not liked in Germany. My father said that the Grubers "paraded"
their Judaism for everyone to see. They wore yarmulkas all the
time. I think my father thought it was arrogant. He always
believed in assimilation. It was a great shock to him when he
too was made to wear a yellow star on his coat and he was
eventually taken away. (*She starts to cry*)

Magda Dr Feldman, is this really necessary?

Dr Feldman (*ignoring Magda*) It's good to talk about these
things. Then one can clear the decks and start a new life.

Anna (*recovering*) Do you do this all the time?

Dr Feldman I talk to survivors like yourself. Yes. It's my job.

Anna (*sarcastically*) I suppose you become hardened to all the
suffering. It must even become boring to listen to so many hard
luck stories.

Dr Feldman (*quietly*) No. Never boring. (*He pulls up his shirt
sleeve and shows Anna the number tattooed on his wrist*)
Dachau.

Anna I'm sorry. I didn't realize ...

Dr Feldman That's why I'm so well-suited to this job. You were
telling me about your marriage.

Anna Yes. My marriage. I loved Joseph passionately but he always made me feel inadequate.

Dr Feldman Why?

Anna Because he was so good. He was so full of principles. I'm making him sound like a pompous bore, but he wasn't like that. He was a genuinely good man. Full of compassion and full of energy. He helped many Jews to hide, or escape. He worked for an organization which sent Jewish children abroad, early in the war. I think they were smuggled to England. God will bless him for that. But, because of his activities he put himself and all his family, my family too, in danger. The Nazis came one night and took us all. His parents lived in the apartment above us. We were all taken to the railway station and there I saw my parents, frightened and huddled together in another group. My father shouted abuse at Joseph across the heads of the people. He could not forgive him, he said, for what he had done to us. (*She starts to cry again*) That was the last I saw of him.

Magda Dr Feldman, please.

Dr Feldman Magda, if you continue to interfere, you will be sent from the room.

Anna It's all right. I'm all right. Stay, Magda. Maybe you and I will learn something.

Dr Feldman How will you learn something, Anna?

Anna (*smiling*) I lost my identity, Doctor. Maybe I never really had one. I tried to be Jewish for a few years and then I tried to be a human being. The trouble is that by the time I had learnt to be a Jew I had become something less than human. Thus proving their theory.

Magda Whose theory?

Anna The Nazis. They believed that Jews and Slavs and gypsies were sub-human and — somewhere along the line — I grew to believe that too.

Magda You don't mean that!

Anna Tell her, Dr Feldman. Tell her how we all became animals in the camps.

Dr Feldman Not everyone did. There were many acts of human kindness.

Anna Yes. Perhaps there were. But they were far outweighed by the acts of bestiality.

Magda The Nazis were the animals, not the inmates.

Anna No. You don't understand. Of course the Nazis were vile, but you knew where you were with them. It was the woman in the bed next to you or the man who doled out the food for the block ... It was what we were talking about earlier — what people do to survive. That was the greatest shock to me. I had accepted that I was Jewish and that made me different from other Germans and so then I looked for some kind of cameraderie amongst my fellow Jews. It wasn't there. I learnt to trust no-one. It was a terrible, terrible isolation.

Dr Feldman (*looking at his notes again*) The letter from your doctor in Munich says that you were sterilized. Is that correct?

Anna Yes.

Dr Feldman I have to ask you this, I'm sorry. Was the — operation — done without anaesthetic?

Anna No.

Dr Feldman (*surprised*) No? But all the female sterilizations in Thereisenstadt were done without pain relief. This much we know.

Anna I wasn't operated on in that place. It was — somewhere else — I don't remember ——

Dr Feldman But you know that it was done with an anaesthetic?

Anna (*irritably*) Yes. Is it important that you know?

Dr Feldman I'm sorry. My report has to go to some people who are hunting down Nazi war criminals. They have been successful in finding some of the doctors who performed such operations and want to prosecute them — with the help of victims like yourself.

Anna I can't help you. I don't want to be involved in such proceedings.

Dr Feldman Why did you specifically request that you should not be examined by a doctor in this country? It has caused some problems with your immigration application.

Anna I have the right to be left alone. I've had enough of doctors to last me a lifetime. My doctor in Munich said that all you required was a blood test, if she fully examined me and sent a full report.

Dr Feldman Yes. I suppose so. But tell me — why was the Munich doctor's examination acceptable to you and not one of our doctors? Was it because she was a woman? We could have found a woman doctor here for you.

Anna She was a good woman. I trusted her. It's very hot in here.

Magda I'm sorry, we can't open the window at the moment. There was a bomb explosion across the street yesterday. I'll go and get you some summer clothes. We have a storeroom downstairs.

Anna No! It's not important!

Magda I won't be a minute.

Magda exits

Anna (*agitatedly*) It's not important! Tell her to come back!

Dr Feldman Are you worried about being left alone with me?

Anna looks puzzled, then laughs

Anna No, Doctor, I'm not afraid of being alone with a man.

Dr Feldman You seemed concerned about Magda leaving. I just wondered if that was the problem.

Anna No.

There is silence for a while

Dr Feldman Tell me some more about your husband.

Anna Joseph? What can I tell you? He is — was — very handsome, very intelligent. As I said before, a good man.

Dr Feldman Did you love him?

Anna Passionately. Intensely. (*Flatly*) He was a very good lover.

Dr Feldman He has talked about nothing but you for the last two months.

Anna Has he.

Dr Feldman Your reaction to the news that he is alive is rather curious. I have seen many reactions, ranging from hysteria and tears to violent hatred when spouses have been told that their partner is alive — but nothing like yours.

Anna And how would you describe my reaction?

Dr Feldman At first you were shocked, but now you seem indifferent — perhaps a little fearful.

Anna Wouldn't you be afraid of meeting someone that you loved very much, after everything we have been through?

Dr Feldman I might be, if I were not the person I was claiming to be ...

Anna (*laughing sarcastically*) Oh I see, that's your game. You think I'm an impostor!

Dr Feldman I keep an open mind on these matters. I just find your reactions a little curious, that's all, and you must admit that your whereabouts over the last ten years have been a little vague.

Anna I haven't changed that much physically. My soul has died, which reflects in my eyes and a little round my mouth. Surely Joseph has told you, from my immigration photograph, that it's me?

Dr Feldman He hasn't seen your photograph. Besides, we know that photographs can lie.

Anna (*looking at Joseph's photograph again*) Joseph has changed a great deal. (*She goes to her handbag and produces a very* *small and battered photograph from it*) That's how he used to look, when we married. There we are ... the two of us together. Two different people, in a different world. (*She shows the photograph to Dr Feldman*)

Dr Feldman (*looking at the photograph*) You're right. You haven't changed much. I'll have to keep this photo ...

Anna No! It's the only thing I have to remind me. I kept it through all the camps.

Dr Feldman It will be returned. Besides, you will have Joseph soon. That's better than a photograph, surely?

Anna (*becoming hysterical*) I want that photograph back! It's mine! I want it!

Dr Feldman (*giving the photograph back to Anna*) All right, Anna. It's all right. Here is the photo.

Anna It's all I have! It's all I have! (*She sobs*)

Magda enters, carrying a low cut summer dress

During the following, Dr Feldman takes a syringe from his briefcase and fills it from a bottle

My Joseph has gone — my young and strong man. It doesn't matter that you've found him again. It's not the same. There's too much happened ...

Dr Feldman Magda. (*He motions to Magda to roll up Anna's sleeve and hold her*)

Anna sees Dr Feldman's gesture and throws herself across the room against the wall

Anna No!

Dr Feldman and Magda follow Anna

Dr Feldman This is just to calm you down, Anna, it won't hurt. (*He approaches Anna and tries to take hold of her*)

Anna (*fighting him*) No! No! No drugs! Get off me, you Nazi pig!

Dr Feldman succeeds in injecting Anna

Dr Feldman There. It's all right, Anna. No-one is going to hurt you. This will help you rest. Let's get you on to the bed. Magda, help me.

Dr Feldman and Magda help the weeping Anna on to the bed

Magda Ssh. Ssh. (*She strokes Anna's forehead*) Let's make you more comfortable. I've brought a dress for you. (*She starts to undo Anna's blouse*)

Anna (*grabbing Magda's hand*) No! Don't touch me!

Magda But I'm only going to change your clothes for you. You're hot in those things. Look! (*She picks up the dress and shows it to Anna*) This is nice and light. You'll be cooler.

Anna I won't wear it. Leave me alone.

Dr Feldman Leave it for the moment, Magda. Let the sedative take effect.

Anna (*struggling to sit upright in the bed*) I won't let you take my clothes off when I'm asleep. I can fight these drugs. I've had them before.

Dr Feldman No-one is going to hurt you, Anna. You're amongst friends, in Israel. No-one is going to hurt you.

Anna Leave me alone.

Dr Feldman Anna. Whatever was done to your body in the camps will not shock us or upset us. Magda and I have seen many scars. There is nothing to feel ashamed about.

Anna begins to laugh hysterically but softly, as she is now slipping into sedation

Anna Scars! I'm not worried about scars on my body! I have a good body, Doctor. Even my sterilization was done tastefully, so as not to spoil my body. My body was my salvation.

Dr Feldman Go on ...

Anna Joseph was a good lover and he loved my body. Ecstasy —
   being with Joseph was ecstasy. He was a man who could make
   the physical act truly an act of love.

Dr Feldman (*softly*) It will be like that again.

Anna No. Never again.

Dr Feldman Joseph was not sterilized. He is a fully functioning
   man, if that is what is worrying you.

Anna starts to cry and continues to do so through the following

Anna (*crying*) Oh, God. That makes it worse.

Dr Feldman Why?

Anna Joseph was a good man.

Dr Feldman You keep saying that. Why is it so important to you?

Anna A man of principles, a religious man. Do you know that I
   had to ritually purify myself every month after the curse, before
   he would sleep with me? I wasn't brought up to be orthodox.
   I didn't know women had to do such things.

Magda It's not a shameful thing, Anna. My mother taught me
   that it is beautiful to purify yourself for your husband.

Anna But how do I do it now? Oh, God, tell me how I can make
   myself pure for Joseph? (*She stands, her back to the audience,
   and, with a violent movement, rips her blouse down to her
   waist. She is wearing a brassière under her blouse*) Look! You
   have a number but I have a name. Tattooed across my chest.
   Feldhure. Field whore. And no-one can ever erase it. No man
   can ever look at me without knowing what I have been.

*Magda takes the raincoat off the armchair and wraps it round
Anna. Magda embraces Anna and leads her back to the bed. Dr
Feldman takes a deep breath and moves to pick up his notepad*

Yes. Write that in your report, Doctor. This woman spent four
years in a camp providing sexual services for German soldiers.

She was — had — by half the German army, because she had
blonde hair and a good body and she would do anything to stay
alive. I wish they'd gassed me at Thereisenstadt.

Magda Don't ...

Anna I was a coward. I didn't want to die of starvation or be shot
or gassed. I was young and they offered me a kind of life. I
didn't know that it was a different way to die. Just a simple
operation so that I didn't produce any half-Jewish bastards and
then all I had to do was open my legs ——

Magda Please don't ——

Feldman Let her get it out of her system.

Anna Yes. Out of my system. How do you wipe out four years
of hell? The sex was nothing. A good bath and I was a new
woman. But the abuse — that was something else. I could write
a book, Doctor, on the Nazi mind at work during the act of
copulation with a Jewess. Perhaps all men are like that. Perhaps
even Joseph, when he sees the mark on my chest, will get great
pleasure from physically and mentally humiliating me. Send
the girl away and I'll tell you all the disgusting details.

Dr Feldman Nothing you could tell me would disgust me, Anna.
I'm here to help you. Try to get some rest now. I will stay with
you. (*He draws Magda aside; to her*) Go and fetch her husband
now.

Magda Do you think it's wise, Dr Feldman. She's so upset ...

Dr Feldman I want him here before she slides into
unconsciousness. Can you manage?

Magda Yes.

Magda exits

Dr Feldman Let's talk some more, Anna.

Anna Don't make me tell you about it all. I don't think I could
really face it.

Dr Feldman No, that's all right, Anna. I don't want the details. We'll talk again when you're better about the things that you have to face. You're going to need help to get over the last ten years of your life. My colleagues and I will help you.

Anna I don't need a psychiatrist. I'm not mad.

Dr Feldman Of course you're not. But you have to talk to someone and you won't feel able to tell Joseph for a while.

Anna I won't ever be able to face Joseph. It's better that I go back to Germany.

Dr Feldman No, Anna. That won't solve anything. Joseph still loves you and wants you. I honestly think he would die if you left him now.

Anna You don't understand ——

Dr Feldman I do understand. I have talked to many, many people who have great burdens of guilt to unload. Maybe your Joseph is one of them.

Anna Joseph? He would never do anything to save his own life at the expense of anyone else. I know him.

Dr Feldman Believe me, Anna. The most saintly of people survived the Holocaust by doing the most terrible things. I did.

Anna You?

Dr Feldman Yes, me. (*His voice breaks a little but he doesn't lose control*) I informed on people. I assisted in operations, convincing myself that I might be able to help them. I even stole food from children. I watched others die and just thanked God that it wasn't me. I have much to be ashamed of. When I was liberated I had a breakdown and it was then I learnt that many others were like me. We were reduced to animals and we behaved like them. And I learnt that I couldn't carry the burden of guilt by myself. I had to share it, I had to face up to my crimes and I had to do something to redeem myself. My way was to take on this job. Your way could be to give Joseph back his life again.

Anna How could I ever take him into my arms again? Even if he
were able to forgive me, every time I took my clothes off, it
would be there — the mark of the whore.

Dr Feldman That may not be important. Trust me.

Anna You're not Joseph. You don't know how he would react.

Dr Feldman I probably know him better than you do. I know that
he has done some terrible things himself and feels shame, just
like you.

Anna What did he do?

Dr Feldman Only Joseph can tell you that, when he's ready. And
you will tell him your story, when you are ready.

Anna My story is here for everyone to see. I can't wait for the
right moment, Doctor.

Dr Feldman Maybe you can. Trust me.

Magda enters, pushing Joseph in a wheelchair. Joseph is blind

Joseph.

Anna (*trying to get off the bed and hide*) Oh, God! No! I'm not
ready!

Dr Feldman Courage, Anna. I told you to trust me.

Joseph Anna? Anna, is it really you?

Anna (*keeping her back to Joseph*) Y—yes, Joseph. It's me!

Joseph Magda, take me over there.

*Magda wheels Joseph over to Anna's side. Joseph takes Anna's
hand. Anna tries not to look at Joseph but it is a great torment. She
is holding back tears*

Anna. My Anna. (*He buries his face in her skirt and cries softly*)

Anna puts her hand on his hair and strokes it

(*Raising his head*) Kneel down, Anna, so that I can feel your
face.

Anna's face registers that she realizes that Joseph is blind. She slowly kneels down, letting the raincoat slip from her shoulders. The tattoo is visible on her chest above her brassière

Anna Joseph ... you're blind ...
Joseph It doesn't matter. I can see you through my fingers. Anna, you haven't changed.
Anna (*running her fingers over the tattoo and not looking at Dr Feldman*) Thank you, Doctor. (*She takes Joseph's hand and puts it on her chest*) I have some scars ...

Joseph's hand glosses over the tattoo and back up her neck to her face

Joseph Nothing is changed, Anna ...

CURTAIN

FURNITURE AND PROPERTY LIST

On stage :   Bed
Table. *On it*: gas mask container
Two armchairs
Coffee table. *On it*: ashtray

Off stage :   Automatic rifle (**Magda**)
Raincoat. *In pocket*: packet of cigarettes, lighter
(**Anna**)
Briefcase. *In it*: papers, notepad, pen, photograph,
newspaper, hypodermic syringe, bottle of
sedative (**Dr Feldman**)
Handbag. *In it*:photograph (**Anna**)
Small suitcase *In it*: clothes (**Anna**)
Tray. *On it*: tea cups, saucers, teapot, milk jug etc.
(**Magda**)
Low cut summer dress (**Magda**)
Wheelchair (**Joseph**)

LIGHTING PLOT

Practical fittings required: nil

To open: General interior lighting

No cues

Printed by
THE KINGFISHER PRESS, LONDON NW10 6UG